Yours, Mine, & Ours

A Cookbook

By

R. Bruce Laudermilk

ISBN: 1-4033-0200-6 (ebook)
ISBN: 1-4033-0201-4 (softcover)

Library of Congress Control Number: 2002090409

This book is printed on acid free paper.

Printed in the United States of America
Bloomington, IN

1stBooks – rev. 03/28/02

Acknowledgements

A warm thank you goes to my wife Cindy for her patience over the years of this book being worked on. A thank you goes to my daughters Ashley, and Amanda for without the use of their computers I would only have hand written notes.

Contents

Soups & Sauces

Entrees

Rice, Pasta, Vegetables

Desserts & Other Things

Cooking Basics and Theory

Roasting: To cook in a moderate oven 250 to 325 degrees F. (the lower temperature will increase the yield of the finished product, but will increase the roasting time.) For larger or tougher cuts of meat.

Place the mirepoix in the bottom of the pan, place item to roast on top, place in oven till desired doneness.

Save the drippings for sauce or gravy.

Before carving or slicing any roast item let it sit for 15 to 20 minutes to let the natural juices within redistribute through out.

Broiling: To cook with high heat 500 to 700 degrees F. Only tender cuts of meat are suitable with moderate amount of marbling. Cook to desired doneness. With broiling the heat comes from the top.

Grilling: The heat comes from the bottom 300 to 450 degrees F. With the lower temperatures a variety of items can be grilled. (turkeys, hams, fish, vegetables ect…)

Sautéing: Means to jump.

A way of cooking, to fry lightly but quickly in a small amount of fat. Smaller cuts of meat or seafood. The meat or seafood is usually dusted lightly with flour just before being sautéed, if not it should be patted dry. To much product in the pan at one time will slow down the cooking process and cause excessive moisture in the pan. Sauces can be made from drippings or juice in the pan.

Pan Frying: Similar to sautéing but it is different. Pan frying is using larger cuts of meat or seafood coated with some type of breading or flour and placed in a pan with moderate amount of hot fat. In some recipes the product is only cooked to color (golden brown) and finished in the oven. A sauce <u>cannot</u> be made from the pan on this type of item.

Deep Fat Frying: The meat or seafood is coated with some type of breading and immersed completely in shortening and cooked till golden brown and done. If a sauce is to accompany the fried product it should be served with the fried product on top of the sauce or on the side.

Poaching: To simmer in a flavored liquid at a temperature of 205 degrees F.

Items are cooked with some type of acid to aid in protein coagulation or in a court bouillon.

Boiling: (simmering)
Water or very light stock used primarily for vegetables, 212 degrees F.
This method is not good for large cuts of meat, as it tends to make the item very tough.

Simmering: This is the method most preferred for large cuts of meat and is cooked at a temperature of 205 to 210 degrees F. to keep the item from becoming tough. Example: corned beef brisket, pot roast.
To check for doneness of a simmering item a skewer can be inserted to check for tenderness of the item. Easy insertion means the item is done. If it goes in with difficulty the item must cook longer as it is not done.

Braising: To sear a product keeping the maximum amount of juice in the product, and finished by a moderate amount of hot liquid but, not to immerse completely with the liquid and then placed into the oven within a tightly covered dish or Dutch oven.

Searing: A product is placed in a very hot pan turned frequently and quickly to seal in all the juices.

Stewing: The product is seared and then covered completely with hot liquid and cooked at a temperature not to exceed 185 to 190 degrees F. to allow meat to become tender.

Thickening Agents
most commonly used

Thickening Agents: A wide variety of items can be used to thicken soups, sauces, and gravies. Some will thicken when cold, while most thicken only when hot.

Roux: Half fat / shortening and half flour cooked on moderate heat

> 3 to 5 minutes for white roux
> 5 to 9 minutes for blond roux
> 10 to 15 minutes for brown roux

Above rouxs: Must be cooked at a moderate heat
    The darker the roux, the more roux is required to thicken the same amount.

To Thicken: (1 quart / 4 cups)
> **Light:** 2 oz. flour - 2 oz. fat
> **Medium:** 3 oz. flour - 3 oz. fat
> **Thick:** 4 oz. flour - 4 oz. fat
> Cream Soups 3 oz. flour - 3 oz. fat

White Wash: 1/3 flour mixed with 2/3 cold water.
Corn Starch: Mixed with cold water, juice, or a stock.

Other Thicking Agents Include: Agar-agar, arrowroot, rice flour, corn flour, liaisons, breads, beurre manie, potatoes, rice, and pasta's

With the use of any thickening agent, the liquid it is to be added with should be hot but not boiling, so as not to have lumps, add it slowly while mixing thoroughly.

Variety of Cuts often used

Name	Size of Cut
Brunoise	1/8"x 1/8"x1/8"
Fine Dice	1/4"x 1/4"x 1/4"
Medium	1/2"x 1/2"x 1/2"
Large Dice	3/4"x 3/4"x 3/4"
Paysanne	1/2"x 1/2"x 1/8"
Battonnette	1/4"x1/4"x 1-11/2"
Julienne	1/8"x 1/8"x 1-11/2"
Farmers Cut	3/4" triangles
Oriental / Bias Cut	1"-2" long, cut on a slant

Various Different Types of Metal Used for Cooking;
Pots, Pans ect...
In order of best to least conductive

Copper: The best, but due to expense not very economical.

Aluminum: Heat is evenly distributed on the cooking surface.

Aluminum /w Teflon: Very good due to the Teflon's non-stick surface, wide variety of pan types.

Calapon: Dark grey or black, heavy metal pans in which the non-stick surface is throughout the pan. Great pans, but expensive.

Cast Iron: Good, but will have hot spots on cooking surface. Very high maintenance to keep from rusting. **Must Be Well Seasoned !** To some cast iron is a healthier way to cook.

Stainless Steel: A easy material to keep clean but heat goes directly through and will burn easily.

The heavier or thicker the bottom of the pan the more evenly the heat from below will be distributed.

Basic Kitchen Tools

Measuring Spoons
Measuring Cups - from 1/8 cup up to 2 cups
Wire Whisks - Large, Medium, and Small
Rubber Spatulas - various sizes and lengths
Pancake Spatula
Tongs - Lengths of 6" and 8"
Spoons - Perforated and solid
Roast Fork (2 tongs)
Paring Knife - 4-6"
Utility Knife - 6-8"
French Knife - 8-10"
Roast Slicer - 10-12"
Serated Slicer - 10-12"
Knife Sharpening Steel - 10-12"
Vegetable Peeler
Rolling Pin - Medium Size
Sauce Pans w/lids - 1 qt and 2 qt
Stock Pot - 6-8 qt w/lid
Sautee Pans - 6",8",10",12"
Collander/Vegetable/ Pasta Strainer - Large and Small
Cutting Boards - Large and Small
Broiler Pan
Cake Pans - 8"x8" and 13"x9"
Soup Laddle - 2oz, 6oz, 8oz
Probe Thermometer

Average Cooking Losses

ROASTING: the amount of loss through roasting depends mainly on the method applied.

LOW HEAT MEANS ~ LESS SHRINKAGE

ITEM	COOKING LOSS
BEEF, prime rib # 109	20%
prime rib, bnls.	20%
top sirloin	25%
round	25%
PORK, fresh ham, bnls.	23%
loins, bnls.	20%
shoulders,	25% to 30%
LAMB, leg, bnls.	29%
shoulder, bnls.	24%
CHICKEN, (depending on fat content)	12 % to 22 %

STEWING, BRAISING OR BOILED

BEEF, lesser grades	30% to 35 %
PORK, lesser grades	32 % to 36 %
CHICKEN,	15 % to 20 %

Fresh Vegetable Buying

FRESHNESS — Fresh vegetables are living, breathing organisms. Their life processes continue after the harvest up until they die and decay. Like many living things they use oxygen and give off heat.

PRICE — The best buyer, is the one who buys vegetables that are best suited to the particular use. Price needs to be balanced against such factors as freshness, tenderness, appearance, size and shape of the product to be purchased.

SEASONAL — Most vegetables have seasonal changes that they go through, yet many are available year round. A careful eye is needed when you buy early or late in the particular season.

PACKAGING— Vegetables are available in a wide variety of consumer packaging, with some even going to the size used in hotels and restaurants. Buy in a size that you will be using within a few days, not all bulk packaging is a good price value if some goes to waste.

PARTIALLY
PREPARED — Local grocery stores now offer a wide selection of fresh
VEGETABLES vegetables in a prepared form and some are ready to use. These items are sometimes a great time saver and are of very good quality.

HANDLING
CARE — All vegetables should be handled with care. They do need good ventilation space, do not tightly stack together, because they are a living, breathing thing and you will shorten the life of your vegetables along with reducing the quality.

Measurements // Abbreviations

tsp. = teaspoon
Tbsp = tablespoon
oz. = ounce
c = cup
pt. = pint
qt. = quart
gal. = gallon
lb. = pound

3 tsp = 1tbsp
2 Tbsp = 1 oz.
8 oz. = 1 c
2 c = 1 pt. = 16 oz.
2 pt. = 1 qt. = 32 oz.
4 qt. = 1 gal. = 128 oz.
16 oz. = 1 lb.
8 lb. = 1 gal.

Weights and Measures
commonly used

ITEM	1 Tablespoon ounces	1 Cup ounces	ITEM	1 Tablespoon ounces	1 Cup ounces
Apples, diced fresh		4	Flour, all purpose	1/4	3-7/8
Bacon, diced raw	1/2	8	Honey	5/8	11
Bacon, diced cooked		6	Lettuce, shredded		2
Baking Powder	1/2	6	Mayonnaise	1/2	8
Baking Soda	1/2	6	Meat ground raw	1/2	8
Beans, dry asst.		7	Meat, ground cooked	1/2	8
Bread Crumbs, dry	1/4	4	Meat, diced cooked	1/3	5-1/3
Bread Crumbs, moist	1/8	2	Milk, dry		4
Butter	1/2	8	Milk, whole		8-1/4
Carrots, diced		5	Molasses	3/4	12
Celery, diced	1/4	4	Nuts, ground	1/2	4-1/4
Cheese, shredded	1/4	4	Nuts pieces	1/2	4
Cheese, Cottage	1/2	8	Oats, rolled		3
Chocolate, grated	1/4	4	Oils, asst.	1/2	8
Chocolate, melted	1/2	8	Onions, diced raw	1/4	4
Cocoa, powder	1/4	3-1/2	Parsley, chopped fresh	3	
Coconut, grated		2-1/2	Peanut Butter		9
Coconut, shredded		2-1/2	Peppers, green diced	1/4	4
Corn Meal		5	Potatoes, diced cooked		6-1/4
Cornstarch	1/3	5-1/3	Raisins, seedless		5-1/2
Cracker Crumbs	1/4	4	Rice, raw	1/2	8
Egg Whites(8)approx.		8	Salt	1/2	8
Egg Yokes (12)approx.		8	Spices, ground asst.	1/8	2
Egg Whole, w/o shell (5)approx.	1	8	Sugar, Brown	1/2	7
Farina		6-1/4	Sugar, Confectioners	1/4	4-3/4
Flour, cake(sifted)	1/4	3-7/8	Sugar, Granulated	1/2	8
Flour, Bread(sifted)	1/4	4-1/4	Syrup, Corn	3/4	11

Can Sizes and Volume

CAN #	=	FLUID OZ. VOLUME	=	CUPS approx.
6		4 3/4		1/2
303, also #1		15.6		2
303, cylinder		19.0		2 1/3
2		19.9		2 1/2
2, cylinder		23.0		3.
2 1/2		28.5		3 1/2
5		56.0		7.
10		103.7		12 3/4
1 gallon		128		16

Scoop Sizes

SCOOP SIZES	MEASURE / TBSP.	APPROX. WEIGHT #
30	2	1 to 1 1/2 ounces
24	2 2/3	1 1/2 to 1 3/4 ounces
20	3	1 3/4 to 2 ounces
16	4	2 to 2 1/4 ounces
12	5	2 1/2 to 3 ounces
10	6	3 1/2 to 4 ounces
8	8	4 1/2 to 5 ounces

Calibrating a Probe Thermometer

When calibrating thermometer, handle it gently, because rough handling or dropping will cause it to lose calibration.

WHEN: Calibrate each thermometer frequently. Weekly or at least once a month, or after a thermometer has been dropped.

HOW: 1.   Fill a medium-sized glass with ice.
Add water to ice.
Place thermometer in glass of ice water.
2.   Wait 3 minutes.
Stir water occasionally.
3.   After 3 minutes, thermometer should read 32 degrees F.

WHO: Each chef or cook doing food preparation of potentially hazardous foods should have access to a probe thermometer.

— CORRECTIVE ACTION —

If a thermometer does not read 32 degrees F. after it has been in ice water for 3 minutes:

1.   Leave it in the ice water.
2.   Using pliers, 7/16" wrench, or adjustable wrench, turn the adjustable nut on the back of the thermometer until the needle reads 32 degrees F.
It may be necessary to add more ice.
3.   Wait 3 minutes, stir occasionally.
4.   After 3 minutes, the thermometer should read 32 degrees F.
If not, repeat corrective action.

How To Make the Pyramid Work for You

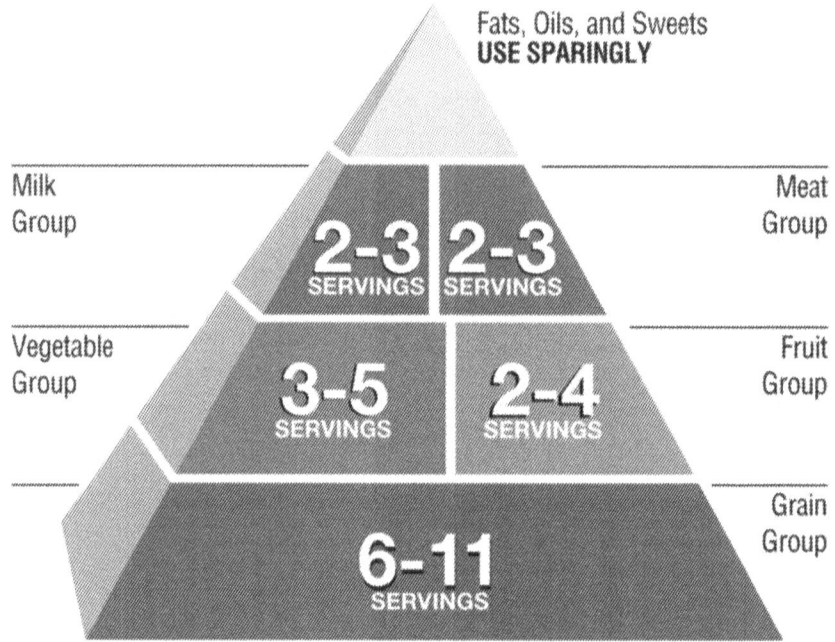

Fats, Oils, and Sweets
USE SPARINGLY

Milk Group

Meat Group

Vegetable Group

Fruit Group

Grain Group

2-3 SERVINGS 2-3 SERVINGS

3-5 SERVINGS 2-4 SERVINGS

6-11 SERVINGS

Food Guide Pyramid

USE THE FOOD GUIDE PYRAMID TO HELP YOU EAT BETTER EVERY DAY

The dietary guidelines way. Start with plenty of breads, cereals, rice, and pasta: vegetables: and fruits. Add two or three servings from the milk group and two to three servings from the meat group.

Each one of these food groups provides some, but not all, of the nutrients you need. No one food group is more important than another. For good health you need them all. Go easy on fats, oils, and sweets, the foods in the small tip of the PYRAMID

SOURCE: U.S. Department of Agriculture /U.S. Department of Health and Human Services

Herb's & Spices

Herb's and Spices history goes back many, many centuries to the earliest of times, and have many uses; foods, beverages, medicinal, and soothing teas.

Some of the folk lores and herbal medicines used years gone by are truly worth reading about.

The amounts of herb's and spices used in a recipe can vary depending upon your own tastes and liking.

Become adventurous in tasting and trying a variety of herb's and spices.

Folk - Lore

Basil — Settling of stomach

Bay Leaf— Strength to digestion

Celery Seed—Stimulant, liver troubles, nervousness.

Dill— Stimulant, stomach remedy, colic in children, quieting to nerves when taken in warm milk, stops hiccups.

Ginger—Sore throat when chewed, good for diarrhea, colds.

Marjoram— Good for loss of appetite, cough, tooth ache, head ache.

Nutmeg—Expectorant, prevents gas, intoxicant.

Parsley— Fevers, kidney stones, liver

Sage— As a gargle for sore throat (tea), stomach, liver, kidneys, soothing for nerves, should stop the flow of mothers milk.

Thyme— Good for fevers, decreases nightmares, asthma, lung trouble, cramping of the stomach, cold relief, headaches.

Peppermint— Stimulant, chills, colic, fever, dizziness, gas on stomach, nausea, vomiting, diarrhea, headaches.

Spearmint— Colic, gas, kidneys, bladder, excellent for morning sickness, soothes nerves.

Herb's & Spices

Allspice-Known outside the United States as pimento, it is the dried unripe berry of the pimenta dioica. It is a medium-sized ever green tree 25-40 feet tall. Called this due to it's flavor, which resembles a blend of cinnamon, nutmeg and cloves.

Anise Seed- An annual herb of the parsley family 2-3 feet tall.

Aromatic seed, a strong licorice like flavor and odor.

Star Anise-Small evergreen tree native to Southwestern China, hard brown fruit if let to bloom. Shape to be that of a star. Licorice like flavor and odor.

Basil-Known also as sweet basil, an annual herb of the mint family, aromatic and sweet smelling leaves.

Bay Leaves (laurel)-A evergreen member of the laurel family. Grows to a height of 50-60 feet, a bitter spicy flavor.

Capsicum Peppers-A family name for a wide variety of peppers, consisting of paprika, cayenne and chili peppers. Piquant spice when dried and ground. Each type has it's own distinct flavor and aroma.

Caraway Seed- The seed is the fruit of a hardy biennial herb.
A black seed whose odor and taste are between anise and fennel.
Most rye bread uses caraway seed rather than rye seeds.

Cardamom- Is a tall herbaceous perennial, belonging to the ginger family.
Aromatic seeds.

Celery Seed-Dried fruit of a biennial herb of the parsley family, most commonly from a wide variety of wild celery.

Chervil- Small, low growing annual of the parsley family. It is sweeter and more aromatic than parsley.

Cinnamon- Cinnamon and Cassia are of some of the oldest spices known to man, yet the tastes are similar they are different. Most cinnamon in the United States is Cassia.

Cinnamon: A moderate sized bushy evergreen tree of the laurel family. Ceylon is the principal country producing high quality cinnamon.

Cassia: An evergreen of the laurel family native to Vietnam and Eastern Himalayas.
It's thicker bark is better yielding than true cinnamon. It has a more intense aroma and higher oil content.

Cloves- Of the myrtle family, a small evergreen tree, it produces nail shaped flower buds. Very aromatic with a hot spicy flavor.

Coriander Seed- A green, shiny plant which grows 2-3 feet tall. A annual herb of the parsley family.

Cumin Seed- A small annual herb of the parsley family. A strong aromatic, hot and bitter taste.

Dill-A medium sized herb with small feathery leaves, and yellow flowers, dill is related to anise. Can use the leaves or seeds for all types of cooking. Used heavily in the pickle industry.

Fennel- A tall, hardy, aromatic perennial of the parsley family. A wide variety of uses for the entire plant and seeds.

Ginger-A root -stock of a tropical plant is an erect perennial herb 2-4 feet tall.
Long cultivated by the ancient Chinese and Hindus.

Horseradish- A hardy perennial plant of the mustard family. It produces stout white fleshy, cylindrical roots. Highly pungent, penetrating odor, plus volatile oils that cause tears to flow.

Marjoram- Belongs to the mint family, often interchanged with oregano even though they are different in taste. Sweet mint flavor and aroma.

Mint Leaves- There are many species of mint. Primarily peppermint and spearmint.
Both are hardy perennial herb's. Mint goes back many centuries for a variety of uses.

Mustard Seed- Most prominent are yellow or white mustard, they are herbaceous annuals, the demand is high.

Nutmeg ~~ Mace- The nutmeg tree produces two separate spices. A densely foliated evergreen tree. Both spices of which are very aromatic, sweet and highly spicy.
Nutmeg tends to be sweeter and more delicate in aroma than mace.

Oregano- Belongs to the mint family, also called wild marjoram.

Bitter mint flavor and aroma.

Onion Family
Garlic ~~ Onions ~~ Chives
All are belonging to the lily family. This bulbous plant is characterized by their penetrating pungent aroma. Garlic being the strongest and chives being much milder.
There are a great many different varieties to chose from, mostly your tastes will help you decide which to buy and use.

Parsley- A hardy, biennial grows up to 2 feet tall. There are many varieties cultivated
It has a large spectrum of use fresh or dried.

Pepper- This is prepared from small, round berries of a woody perennial evergreen climbing vine. Black and White pepper are of the most used types.
The peppers are characterized by a penetrating odor and hot, biting, and pungent flavor.

Poppy Seed- A robust annual belonging to the poppy family.
The tiny poppy seeds, have an agreeable nutty flavor.

Rose Mary- A small evergreen shrub of the mint family native to the Mediterranean region. Small, narrow, aromatic leaves resembles curved pine needles when dried, used as a seasoning herb.

Saffron- Dried stigmas of the crocus family. This is the most expensive of all spices world wide. Wildly used as a yellowish-orange natural food dye. Very highly aromatic, thread like, dark orange to reddish brown strands of about one inch long.

Sage- An evergreen shrub of the mint family. Dried sage is highly aromatic and fragrant, the taste is pungent and slightly bitter.

Tarragon- A small herbaceous perennial plant of the sunflower family.
The leaves can be used fresh or dried. Its bitter sweet flavor makes it one of the popular herb's in Europe. The aroma is anise like.

Thyme- A diminutive perennial herbaceous shrub of the mint family.
Fresh or dried its uses are unlimited.

Tea Know How
What The Words on a Package of Tea Mean

GREEN, OOLONG, BLACK—These words indicate the way in which the plucked leaves were treated to produce manufactured tea. Black tea is wholly withered and fully fermented; Oolong partly withered and partly fermented; Green is neither withered nor fermented but steamed briefly then dried.

ASSAM, DARJEELING, LAPSANG,
KEEMUN, CEYLON, JAVA —ect..., Refer to the country or district within a country where the tea was grown. Each district is know for the distinctive flavor of it's tea.

ORANGE, PEKOE, SOUCHONG,
FANNINGS, and DUST —are some of the words which indicate the size of the pieces of tea leaf. These words are used to describe black tea. Orange pekoe is the largest grade of black tea, dust is smallest.

GUNPOWDER, PEA LEAF, IMPERIAL
YOUNG HYSON and HYSON—are some of the words which describe the size gradings for green teas.

BROKEN ORANGE PEKOE, BROKEN PEKOE,
BROKEN ORANGE PEKOE SOUCHONG,
FANNINGS, DUST —are some of the words which describe the sizes of broken grades of tea.

THE SMALLER GRADES OF TEA DO NOT HAVE INFERIOR FLAVOR. THEY BREW MORE QUICKLY AND PRODUCE A STRONGER BREW BECAUSE OF GREATER EXPOSURE OF THE LEAF CELLS TO THE BOILING WATER. FOR THIS REASON THE SMALLER GRADES OF TEA ARE USED FOR TEA BAGS.

DIFFERENT KINDS OF TEA

There are about 3000 varieties of tea. Their differences are determined by the plants themselves, by geography and the methods of processing the leaves.

THE PLANTS: The botanical name for the tea bush, THEA SINENSIS, means "devine herb ". There are two main varieties of THEA SINENSIS, "Bohea and Viridis".

Bohea is a Chinese word wu-i, pronounced by some Chinese bu-i, the name of the hills where this shrub was originally grown. viridis means green.

GEOGRAPHY: The principal countries growing tea are India and Ceylon. before 1877, "tea " meant only china tea, but today no figure for Chinese tea production is available.

Tea is often named after the district where it is grown within a country, such as: ASSAM, DARJEELING, LAPSANG, JAVA.
Each produces it's own distinct flavor.

GLOSSARY OF LABEL TERMS

ASSAM; A rich black tea from ASSAM, Northern India. Brewed, it has a heavy reddish color.

BASKET FIRED JAPAN; Describes a Japanese process for toasting and drying tea in baskets made of bamboo. A superb tea which produces a mellow, sparkling brew.

CHINA; Means tea from Formosa, as the U.S. does not import tea from China at this time.

DARJEELING; A black, very fine and full-bodied tea picked only a few months out of the year. It grows at 7000 feet above sea level, near Darjeeling, India.
It is brought to lower levels for processing by means of ropeways or "shoots".

EARL GREY; Is an aromatic blend of Darjeeling, Ceylon and Formosa black teas with unique distinctive flavor. It is named after Earl Grey, Prime Minister of Britain in 1830. The recipe is supposed to have been given to an Emissary of Earl Grey's by a grateful mandarin.

ENGLISH BREAKFAST; Exceptionally fine flavored India and Ceylon black teas, full strong flavor. Good for morning or afternoon.

FORMOSA OOLONG; Tea from Formosa which has been prepared in the "oolong" manner, i.e. partly withered and partly fermented. produces a medium - strength brew with spicy flavor, reminiscent of sun- ripened peaches. Excellent with desserts and pastries. The word "oolong" means black dragon to Europeans, but red dragon to chinese.

HYSON; Is a green tea with a special twist of the leaf. the word is pronounced hi'sn and means "blooming spring " in chinese. " young HYSON "is plucked before the rains and is the earliest part of the crop.

IRISH BLEND; Fine Ceylon and India black teas. Pungent, aromatic brew.

ORANGE PEKOE; Black teas from India and Ceylon.
Does not refer to color of the brew. Some tea authorities say orange blossoms were added to the tea when packed, others say orange refers to the golden color of the tip leaves. Orange pekoe tea was once made from the first two leaves, the youngest, of the tea bush. Today in India and Ceylon, it is a tea with approximately the same- sized leaves obtained by screening fired tea.

PEKOE; Is pronounced to rhyme with heck-o by the tea trade and by the British, but merriam- webster says it is pronounced peek-o in the U.S. Pekoe means "white down " in chinese and describes the silvery baby fuzz that appears on the underside of the young leaves.

R. Bruce Laudermilk

Coffee Know How
What The Words on a Package of Coffee Mean

MOKA; Small irregular grains, yellowing in color and convex on both sides.

BOURBON; Medium-sized grains, yellowing, oblong.

MARTINIQUE; The biggest grains, rounded at the ends, greenish in color.

WHOLE BEAN; The beans have been roasted but not yet ground.

ROASTED; A process of which varies from brand to brand, but during roasting some use sugar molasses or various other products are sometimes added, to coat the berries. This is allowable by law. This gives the berries a better color and a shiny appearance, prevents the loss of aroma and has a further advantage for the merchant of increasing the weight and, allows him to use inferior quality or damaged grains.

GRIND; A variety of different pre-ground coffees are available at your local grocery store. You can also grind your own at the store or at home.

BEAN; The term used for coffee, which there are a wide range of beans.

INSTANT; Soluble beverage of which was an invention of Mr. G. Washington and marketed in 1909.

COFFEE PLANT; Large evergreen shrub with dark shiny leaves. The cherry-like fruit is soaked, de-pulped, dried and the seed is then polished to remove the parchment-like husk and outer filament. The seeds are then classified as to size and ripeness.

Nacho Cheese Dip
YIELD: 3 CUPS

2 cup (1 lb.)	Velvetta Processed Cheese, cut into 1" cubes
1/4 cup	Green Peppers, diced fine
1 Tbsp.	Jalapeno Peppers, diced fine
1/4 cup	Pimentos, diced fine
1 tsp.	Garlic, chopped fine
1/2 cup	Water

METHOD:

Place all ingredients into a 1 qt. sauce pot, place on a med-high burner, stir frequently until mixture is hot and cheese has melted completely.

Serve hot. Or, thin slightly and serve as a chip dip cold.

French Onion Dip
YIELD: 1 Qt.

3 cup	Sour Cream
3/4 cup	Onions, white, diced fine
1/2 tsp.	Garlic, chopped fine
1 Tbsp.	Worcestershire Sauce
1 each	Beef Bouillon Cube
2 Tbsp.	Water, Hot
1 tsp.	Parsley, chopped fine

METHOD:

In to a mixing bowl place sour cream, onions, garlic, Worcestershire sauce, and parsley mix well.

In to a cup place the hot water and beef bouillon cube and dissolve completely and add to the sour cream mixture and mix well.

Serve chilled and enjoy! Your Chips.

Also good with vegetables as a dip.

B.B.Q. Chicken Wings
YIELD: 24 Wings

1/2 cup	Vegetable Oil
24 each	Chicken Wings
1/2 cup	Green Peppers, diced fine
1/2 cup	Onions, Spanish, diced fine
1 tsp.	Cayenne Pepper, ground
2 cup	B.B.Q. Sauce, Your favorite !!!

METHOD:

Place vegetable oil in a frying pan and place on a med-high burner, heat oil and place 6 chicken wings into the pan fry 2-3 minutes on each side till slightly browned, repeat this process till all wings have been fried. Place cooked wings into a oven-proof baking casserole dish.

In a mixing bowl combine all other ingredients mix well, then pour over top of the wings and place uncovered into a pre-heated 350 degree oven and bake for 30 minutes.

Serve with lots of Napkins and enjoy !!!

Salsa
YIELD: 1 quart

2 cup	Tomatoes, diced small
1 cup	Onions, diced small
1/2 cup	Green Peppers, diced small
1 Tbsp.	Banana Pepper, diced fine
1/4 cup	V- 8 juice
1/8 tsp.	Cumin, ground
1/8 tsp.	Garlic, diced fine
1/8 tsp.	Oregano
1/4 tsp.	Salt

METHOD:

Combine all ingredients together in a mixing bowl mix well with a spoon.

This can be used now but better when stored over night in the refrigerator.

Note: If hotter salsa is desired double the banana peppers.

Guacamole
YIELD: 1 quart

2 cup	Avocado, diced small, pitted and peeled
3/4 cup	Tomatoes, diced small
1/2 cup	Onions, diced small
1/4 cup	Sour Cream
1/8 tsp.	Chili Powder
1/8 tsp.	Cumin, ground
1/8 tsp.	Black Pepper
1 tsp.	Lemon Juice
1/2 tsp.	Salt

METHOD:

Combine all ingredients together in a mixing bowl blend thoroughly, place in the refrigerator for 2-3 hours for the best flavors.

Bleu Cheese Dressing
YIELD: 1 Qt.

2 cup	Mayonnaise
1 cup	Bleu Cheese, crumbled
1 tsp.	Worcestershire Sauce
2 Tbsp.	Lemon Juice
1 cup	Sour Cream
1/4 tsp.	White Pepper, ground
1/4 tsp.	Garlic, chopped fine

METHOD:

Combine all ingredients together in a mixing bowl and mix well. Serve chilled.

Thousand Island Dressing
YIELD: 1 Qt.

3 cup	Mayonnaise
1/2 cup	Ketchup
1/4 cup	Pickle Relish, sweet
1 tsp.	Dry Mustard,
2 each	Eggs, boiled, peeled diced fine
1 tsp.	Worcestershire Sauce
1/8 tsp.	White Pepper, ground
2 Tbsp.	Lemon Juice

METHOD:

Combine all ingredients together in a mixing bowl and mix very well.
Serve chilled.

Vinaigarette Dressing
YIELD: 1 Qt.

2 cup	Salad Oil
1 cup	Olive Oil
3/4 cup	Vinegar, White
1/4 cup	Onion, White, diced fine
2 Tbsp.	Parsley, chopped fine
1/4 tsp.	Basil, chopped fine
1/8 tsp.	Oregano, chopped fine
1/4 tsp.	Black Pepper, ground

METHOD:

Combine all the ingredients together in a mixing bowl mix well. Serve well chilled.

Greek Dressing
YIELD: 1 QT.

1 cup	Red Wine Vinegar
1 cup	Olive Oil
1 cup	Onions, Bermuda, diced fine
1 Tbsp.	Basil, chopped fine
1 Tbsp.	Oregano, chopped fine
1 Tbsp.	Garlic, chopped fine
1 Tbsp.	Parsley, chopped fine
1/8 cup	Parmesan Cheese, grated
1/8 cup	Greek Olives (black olives), whole
1/2 cup	Water, cold
1/2 tsp.	Black Pepper, ground
1 tsp.	Salt

METHOD:

Into a 2 qt. mixing bowl place all the ingredients and mix well. Store in a 1 qt. jar with a lid in refrigerator. Shake very well before serving.

Best if marinated for 2-3 days before use.

Red French Dressing
YIELD: 1 1/2 Qt.

2 each	Eggs, whole
1 qt.	Salad oil
1 cup	Cider vinegar
1 tsp.	Salt
1/2 tsp.	Garlic, chopped fine
1/4 tsp.	White Pepper, ground
3 Tbsp.	Sugar, granulated
2 tsp.	Dry Mustard, ground
2 tsp.	Paprika, ground
1 tsp.	Worcestershire Sauce
1/4 cup	Lemon Juice

METHOD:

Place eggs into mixing bowl mix on med-high speed and slowly add oil and vinegar alternating till amounts are used up, add all other ingredients mixing very well.

Store refrigerated till ready for use.

Antipasto
YIELD: 2 QT.

1 cup	Genoa Salami, sliced 1/8" thick, cut into wedges, bite sized pieces
1 cup	Provolone Cheese, sliced 1/4" thick, cut into wedges, bite sized pieces
1 cup	Broccoli flourettes, 1/2" in size
1 cup	Cauliflower flourettes, 1/2" in size
1 cup	Bermuda Onion, julienne sliced 1-1 1/2" long
1 cup	Black Olives, whole, pitted
1 cup	Green Peppers, julienne sliced 1-1 1/2" long
1 cup	Mushrooms, washed, quartered
1 Qt.	Greek Dressing, (see recipe)

METHOD:

Combine all ingredients together into a large mixing bowl and stir till well mixed.

Marinate for 12 - 24 hours for best results.

Chicken Salad Almondine
YIELD: 6 cups

4 cups (4 breasts)	Chicken Breast, cooked, cooled, diced small
1/2 cup	Celery, diced small
1/4 cup	Onions, diced small
1 cup	Mayonnaise
1/8 tsp.	White Pepper, ground
1/8 tsp.	Salt
1/4 tsp.	Curry Powder, ground
1/4 cup	Almonds, sliced, slightly browned in oven
1 1/2 cup	Green Seedless Grapes, small bunches

METHOD:

Into a large mixing bowl add diced chicken, celery, onions, mayonnaise, and all seasonings mix well, add browned almonds and gently fold into mixture.

Serve cold with seedless grapes as a garnish.

Ham Salad
Yield: 6 cups

3 1/2 cups	Ham, diced small
1 1/2 cups	Mayonnaise or salad dressing
1/4 cup	Sweet Relish
3	Hard boiled eggs, small diced
1 tsp	Dry Mustard
1/4 cup	Onions, diced small
1/4 cup	Celery, diced small

METHOD:

Combine all ingredients in a large bowl. Mixing well. Chill well and serve with lettuce, crackers, on bread, or as an appetizer. KEEP COLD.

Potato Salad
YIELD: 3 lb. (6 cups)

1 1/2 lb.	Potatoes, peeled, diced large, cooked and cooled
1 cup	Onions, diced small
1 cup	Celery, diced small
1 1/2 cup	Mayonnaise
2 Tbsp.	Mustard, salad
1/8 tsp.	White Pepper, ground
1/4 tsp.	Salt
3 each	Eggs, whole, cooked, diced small
1/4 cup	Green Pepper, diced small
1/4 cup	Red Pepper, diced small

METHOD:

Place pre-cooked potatoes into large mixing bowl add all ingredients into bowl and mix well, but do not over mix causing potatoes to break up.

Serve well chilled.

Pasta Salad
YIELD: 5 cups

3 cups	TRI-COLORED Rotoni, cooked, rinsed, & cooled
1/2 cup	Onions, diced small
1/2 cup	Celery, diced small
1/4 cup	Black Olives, sliced
1/2 cup	Salad Oil
1/2 cup	Olive Oil
1/2 cup	White Vinegar
1 Tbsp.	Garlic, diced fine
1 tsp.	Salt
1/2 tsp.	Black Pepper
2 Tbsp.	Parsley, chopped fine

METHOD:

Combine all INGREDIENTS in a large bowl. Mix well and chill.

Great with hard salami or pepperoni, good with garlic bread and tossed salad.

Marinated Fresh Garden Vegetables
YIELD: 2qt.

1 cup	Broccoli, flourettes, tops only about 1/2 inch in size
1 cup	Cauliflower, flourettes, about 1/2 inch in size
1 cup	Cucumbers, peeled, cut in half length-wise, sliced 1/4 inch thick
1/2 cup	Celery, julienne strips, 1- 1 1/2 inch long
1/2 cup	Red Peppers, fresh, julienne strips, 1-1 1/2 inch long
1/2 cup	Green Peppers, julienne strips, 1-1 1/2 inch long
1/2 cup	Onions, Spanish, diced fine
1 cup	Carrots, peeled, cut length-wise, sliced 1/8 inch thick
2 cup	Salad Oil
3/4 cup	White Vinegar
1/2 tsp.	Basil, chopped fine
1/4 tsp.	Oregano, chopped fine
1 Tbsp.	Garlic, chopped fine
1/4 tsp.	White Pepper, ground
1 Tbsp.	Salt

METHOD:

Combine all ingredients together into a large mixing bowl mix till well blended.

Marinate 6 - 8 hours, serve well chilled.

Marinated Cucumber & Onion Salad
YIELD: 5 cups

3 cups	Cucumbers, peeled, cut in half length-wise and deseed, slice 1/4 inch thick
1 cup	Onions, Spanish, julienne sliced 1-1 1/2 inch long
1/8 tsp.	White Pepper, ground
1 tsp.	Salt
3/4 cup	Vinegar, White
1/4 cup	Salad Oil
1 tsp.	Dill Weed, chopped fine
1 Tbsp.	Sugar, granulated

METHOD:

Combine all ingredients together into a large mixing bowl mix very well.

Let marinate for 6-8 hours. Serve well chilled.

Basic Chicken Soup
YIELD: 1 Gallon

2 lbs.	Chicken meat, cooked diced medium
3 cups	Onions, medium diced
2 cups	Celery, medium diced
1 cup	Carrots, medium diced
2	Bayleaves
1/8 tsp.	White pepper, ground
1	Whole clove
1/8 tsp.	Thyme, leaves
8	Chicken bouillon cubes
2 oz.	Butter
3 qts.	Hot water

METHOD:

In a 6 quart pot on medium heat, put butter & vegetables, place a lid on the pot and cook for 5 minutes. Slowly remove lid, being careful of escaping steam, stir. Add all seasonings, bouillon cubes, and chicken meat. Stir and add hot water. Bring to a boil, then reduce heat to a simmer, cook an additional 20 to 30 minutes. Adjust seasonings and serve.

VARIATIONS: 1 cup raw rice with the chicken meat or
1 cup noodles with the chicken meat.

Vegetable Soup
YIELD: 1 Gal. (10 - 12oz. servings)

1/2 cup	Potatoes, diced medium
1 cup	Onions, diced medium
1/2 cup	Celery, diced medium
1/2 cup	Carrots, diced medium
1 cup	Green Cabbage, diced small
1/2 cup	Turnips, diced medium
1/2 cup	Broccoli, flourettes, bite sized
1/2 cup	Cauliflower, flourettes, bite sized
2 each	Bayleafs, whole
1/8 tsp.	Black Pepper, ground
1/2 tsp.	Salt
3/4 cup	Tomato Paste
6 Qt.	Water

METHOD:

Place all vegetables into a 8 quart pot cover with the water place on a medium-high burner and bring to a boil. Add spices and tomato paste stir in very well and reduce the heat to medium-low and simmer till the vegetables are tender approximately 1 1/2 hours. Stir frequently.

Serve with a good French Bread.

Navy Bean Soup
YIELD: 1 gallon

1 lb.	Navy Beans, soaked overnight in refrigerator drain before use in soup
1 cup	Bacon raw, diced small
1 cup	Onions, diced small
1/2 cup	Celery, diced small
1/2 cup	Carrots, diced small
2	Bayleaves
1/8 tsp.	Ground thyme
6 Qts.	Water
1/8 tsp.	Black pepper, ground

METHOD:

In an 8 quart soup pot place bacon on medium high heat, stirring until brown. Add all other ingredients. Stir and bring to a boil. Reduce heat and simmer until beans are tender, stirring frequently. A slow cooker could be used. Cooking on top of stove.

Cooking time on stove top 1 1/2 hour or longer.

New England Clam Chowder
YIELD: 1 Gallon

3 cups	Onions, small dice
2 cups	Celery, small dice
1 cup	Carrots, small dice
1 cup	Bacon, small dice, raw
12 oz.	Butter
3 cups	Flour, all purpose
2	Bayleaves
1/2 tsp.	Thyme, leaf
1/8 tsp.	White pepper
3 cups	Raw potatoes, small dice
3 cups	Clams, chopped
21/2 qts.	Milk, scalded

METHOD:

In a 6 quart pot put bacon, using medium heat. Cook until brown, stirring. Add onions, celery, carrots, bay leaves, thyme, and butter. Cook until vegetables are tender, stirring often. Add flour mixing in completely. Add scalded milk, <u>SLOWLY</u>, while stirring until smooth. Add potatoes and clams, mix well. Simmer until potatoes are tender. Adjust seasoning to taste. Serve.

Cream of Broccoli Soup
YIELD: 4 quarts

2 lbs.	Broccoli, fresh diced medium
2 cups	Onions, diced small
1 cup	Celery, diced small
2 cup	Butter
3 cup	Flour, all purpose
2 each	Bay Leaves
1 each	Clove, whole
1/8 tsp.	Thyme, whole
1/8 tsp.	White Pepper, ground
4 each	Chicken Bouillon Cubes
3 quarts	Milk, hot

METHOD:

Place a 6 quart pot on a medium-high burner, melt butter then add all the vegetables stir well, cook till the broccoli is tender. Add flour and stir very well to blend thoroughly, add all spices, bouillon cubes and slowly add hot milk stirring thoroughly, reduce the burner to medium and simmer 15 - 20 minutes stirring frequently.

Cream of Mushroom Soup
YIELD: 4 quarts 10 - 12oz. servings

5 cups	Mushrooms, sliced fresh, washed
2 cups	Onions, diced fine
1 cup	Celery, diced fine
2 cups	Butter
3 quarts	Milk, hot
3 cups	Flour, all purpose
2 each	Bay Leaves
1 each	Clove, whole
1/8 tsp.	Thyme, whole
3 each	Chicken Bouillon Cubes
1/8 tsp.	White Pepper, ground

METHOD:

Place a 6 quart pot on a medium-high burner, add butter and melt once melted add mushrooms, onions and celery cook for 5-10 minutes stirring frequently when vegetables are tender, add flour and stir until well blended. Add all spices, bouillon cubes and slowly add hot milk while stirring thoroughly, reduce the heat on the burner to medium simmer for 15 - 20 minutes stirring frequently.

French Onion Soup au Gratin
SERVES: 6-10oz crocks

2 lbs. Yellow Onions, sliced
1 oz Salad Oil
1 oz Chicken Base
1 oz Beef Base
1 Bayleaf
1 Clove, Whole
1 Tbsp garlic, chopped fine
4 oz red wine
1 ½ qts water
White pepper to taste
Salt to taste
6 oz Croutons
6 oz Shredded or Sliced Swiss Cheese

METHOD:

Place Salad oil into a 4 qt pan get oil very hot add onions and stir slowly allow onions to become browned but not burnt. Add the red wine stir well. Add chicken base, beef base, spices, and water bring to a boil then reduce heat and allow to simmer for 30 minutes. Adjust salt and pepper at this time.

To serve place 9-10oz of soup into a crock, top with 1 oz of croutons then

Chicken Sauce
YIELD: 2 Quarts

3/4 Cups	Butter
1/2 cups	Onions, diced small
1/4 cup	Celery, diced small
1 whole	Bayleaf
Pinch	Ground thyme
1 Cup	Flour
6	Chicken Bouillon Cubes
2 Qts.	Hot water

METHOD:

Place butter in a saucepan that holds at least 3 quarts. On a medium heat melt butter, add onions, celery, bayleaf, thyme, cloves & white pepper. Cook until onions are transparent add flour and stir. Slowly add hot water & bouillon cubes. Stir until smooth, reduce heat and simmer for 10 or 15 minutes. Strain and serve.

Brown Sauce
YIELD: 2 quarts

1 Cup	Butter
1 Cup	Onions
1/2 Cup	Celery
1/2 Cup	Carrots
1 Whole	Bayleaf
Pinch	Thyme
1 Whole	Clove
1 1/2 Cup	Flour
1/4 Cup	Ham, diced small
5	Beef Bouillon Cubes
2 Qts.	Hot Water
1 Cup	Red Wine

METHOD:

Place butter in a saucepan that holds at least 3 quarts. Melt over medium heat, add onions, celery, and carrots. Cook until carrots start to brown slightly. Add bay leaf, thyme, and clove. Stir well add flour stirring until completely blend. Add ham and tomato paste stir well. Slowly add hot water and bouillon cubes. Stir until smooth add red wine. Stirring bring to a boil. Then reduce heat and simmer for 20 to 30 minutes. Strain sauce and serve.

Marinara Sauce
YIELD: 4 quarts

2 cup	Onion, diced small
1 cup	Celery, diced small
1 cup	Carrots, diced small
3-26 oz. cn	Tomatoes, crushed
3-6 oz. cn	Tomato paste
3 Tbsp.	Garlic, diced fine
1/4 cup	Olive Oil
1 Tbsp.	Basil, whole
1 tsp.	Oregano
1/2 tsp.	Rosemary
2 each	Bay Leaf
1 quart	Water

METHOD:

Place olive oil into an 6 qt. sauce pot turn heat on medium high, when oil is hot add onions, celery and carrots, cook till onions become transparent stirring frequently, then add garlic and tomato paste stirring very well, add tomatoes, spices and water stirring well. Bring to a boil then reduce heat to a simmer. Let simmer for approximately 45 minutes, stirring frequently.

Serve over your favorite pasta, meat, fish or poultry dish.

Cream Sauce
YIELD: 2 Qt.

3/4 cup	Butter
1/2 cup	Onion, diced fine
1 each	Bayleaf, whole
Pinch	Thyme, ground
2 each	Cloves, whole
1 cup	Flour
2 Qt.	Milk, hot

METHOD:

Place butter into sauce pan turn burner on Med- Hi melt butter and add onions, bayleaf, thyme and cloves cook till onions are transparent, add flour and stir well. Slowly add HOT milk while stirring till smooth, reduce heat to Med-Lo simmer 5-10 min. Strain sauce to remove onions and spices, Serve.

White Cheese Sauce
YIELD: 2 Qt.

1/2 cup	Butter
1 cup	Flour
1 1/2 Qt.	Milk, Hot
1 each	Bayleaf, whole
Pinch	Thyme, ground
Pinch	Cayenne Pepper, ground
1 cup	Baby Swiss, shredded
1 cup	Mozzarella, shredded

METHOD:

Place butter into sauce pan turn burner on Med-Hi melt butter and add flour and stir very well, Slowly add HOT milk while stirring till smooth, add Bayleaf, thyme, cayenne pepper and both cheeses stir in well.
Reduce heat to Med- Lo and simmer for 5-10 min. stirring frequently.
Remove Bayleaf before serving.

Yellow Cheese Sauce
YIELD: 2 Qt.

1/2 cup	Butter
1 cup	Flour
1 1/2 Qt.	Milk, Hot
1 each	Bayleaf, whole
Pinch	Cayenne Pepper, ground
Pinch	Thyme, ground
1 1/2 cup	American Cheese, shredded
1/2 cup	Cheddar Cheese, shredded

METHOD:

Place butter into sauce pan turn burner on Med-Hi melt butter and add flour, stir very well. Slowly add HOT milk while stirring till smooth, add Bayleaf, thyme, cayenne pepper and both cheeses stir in well, reduce heat to Med-Lo and simmer for 5- 10 min. stirring frequently. Remove Bayleaf before serving.

Barbecue Sauce
YEILD: 1 quart

1 1/2 cups	Chicken Stock
14 oz.	Catsup, your favorite
1 cup	Tomato Puree
1/2 cup	Onion, medium dice
1 clove	Garlic, fresh
1 each	Lemon, medium size
1/4 cup	Vinegar, cider
1/3 cup	Brown Sugar
1 Tbsp.	Pickling Spice, whole
1 tsp.	Worcestershire Sauce
1/2 tsp.	Tabosco Sauce

METHOD:

Combine all ingredients together into a 2 qt. sauce pot and stir well, turn burner to medium-high stir frenquently bring to a boil, reduce heat to simmer stirring frenquently for 30 minutes. Remove from heat and strain through a strainer into a 1 qt. jar, cool.

When cool place lid on jar and keep refrigerated till ready to use.

Meat Loaf
YIELD: 6 servings

2 1/2 lbs.	Ground Beef, fresh
1/4 cup	Olive Oil
1 cup	Onions, diced small
1 cup	Celery, diced small
3 each	Eggs, whole
1 cup	Bread Crumbs, fresh
1/2 cup	Milk
1/4 tsp.	Thyme
1/4 tsp.	Black Pepper, ground
1/2 cup	Ketchup, for use on top

METHOD: PREHEAT OVEN 350 degrees

Place into the frying pan the olive oil heat up on medium-high, add onions and celery cook till celery and onions are tender, remove from heat and let cool some.

In a mixing bowl mix together ground beef and eggs very well. Add bread crumbs, onions, celery, milk and spices mix till all ingredients are well blended. Form in to a loaf shape and place in a loaf pan place into preheated oven baking for 45 minutes. Remove from oven and spread top with ketchup place back into the oven for 10 minutes, remove and ready to slice and serve.

Chili Con Carne
YIELD:8 servings

2 lbs.	Beef stew meat, 3/4 inch pieces
16 oz.	Onion, medium dice
8 oz.	Green pepper, medium dice
1 -16 oz. cn.	Tomatoes, diced either fresh or canned
4 Tbsp	Flour, all purpose
2	Cloves of garlic, crushed
1/2 tsp.	Oregano, leaf
1/2 tsp. *	Cumin, ground
2 Tbsp.	Chili powder
1/2 tsp.	Salt
4 - 1 lb. cn.	Kidney Beans
2 Tbsp.	Bacon, diced raw

METHOD:

Brown bacon, and add stew meat. Cook until meat is brown, add diced onion and green pepper. Cook until tender. Add all seasonings, garlic and flour. Mix very well. Add diced tomatoes and kidney beans. Mix well and cook in the oven 350 degrees for about and hour. Can be placed in a slow cooker. Making sure meat is tender. Serve hot. Is great with flour tortillas.

* can add more for spicier or less for mild

Beef Stroganoff
YIELD: 6 servings

2 lbs.	Beef, sirloin tips, cut into strips bite size
12 oz.	Onion, medium dice
8 oz.	Celery, medium dice
2 oz.	Butter
3 Tbsp.	Flour, all purpose
2	Beef bouillon, cubes
1/2 tsp.	Worcestershire Sauce
2 cups	Hot water
1 cup	Sour Cream

METHOD:

On medium heat in heavy 6 quart pot, put butter. Melt butter, add beef. Stir until cooked on all sides. Add onion and celery. Cook and stir until tender. Sprinkle flour over cooked mixture, stirring well. Add bouillon cubes and Worcestershire sauce. Slowly add water, stir until smooth. Reduce heat and simmer until meat is tender. Add sour cream, stirring in completely. Serve over noodles or rice.

Hamburger Pie
YIELD: 1 -9 INCH PIE
Serves 6 people

1/2 lb.	Butter or margarine, melted
1 c.	Celery, diced small
1/2 c.	Green pepper, diced small
2 c.	Onions, diced small
3 lbs.	Potatoes, peeled, boiled and mashed
2 lbs.	Ground Beef, cooked drained and seasoned to taste
1 -9 inch	Pie shell, homemade or deep dish frozen, bottom only unbaked

METHOD: PREHEAT OVEN TO 350 degrees.

Place melted butter in sauté pan add celery, pepper, & onions cook until slightly tender. Set aside. Brown beef, season to taste, drain off fat. Boil potatoes until tender mash using a little butter only no other liquid.

Place beef in bottom of pie shell, add vegetables, and top with mashed potatoes. Bake until potatoes are slightly browned. Serve Hot.

Taco Meat
YIELD: 1 lb. cooked

1 lb.	Ground Beef, fresh
1/4 cup	Water
1 cup	Onions, diced fine
1/4 tsp.	Cumin, ground
1/2 tsp.	Oregano
1/2 tsp.	Garlic, diced fine
1 tsp.	Chili Powder

METHOD:

Place ground beef and water into a frying pan turn heat on to medium-high stir the meat very well till all the meat is slightly browned, add onions and spices stir very well reduce the heat to medium cook till onions become transparent and tender.

Beef Burritos
YIELD: 8 each

1 lb.	Taco Meat, hot (see recipe)
1 lb. cn.	Refried Beans, hot
2 cup	Lettuce, shredded fine
2 cup	Cheddar Cheese, shredded (1 cup for use on top)
8 each	Flour Tortillas 12"
1 cup	Sour Cream, for garnish
1 cup	Tomatoes, diced fine, for garnish
1 pint	Salsa, (see recipe)

METHOD:Pre-heat oven at 375 degrees

Place flour tortilla on table place 1/4 cup refried beans in center of tortilla spread out slightly, top this with 1/4 cup taco meat spread out, top this with 1/8 cup of cheddar cheese, then 1/4 cup lettuce spread slightly.

ROLLING METHOD:

Take hold of the top of the tortilla fold towards the center covering the filling, take hold of the left side of tortilla fold towards the center, take the right side of tortilla and fold towards the center.

Now roll the top towards you slowly holding the sides, this now should look like a cylinder shape. The size should be about 6" long and 2-3" in diameter. With practice this will become easy to do.

Place rolled beef burritos on a cookie sheet top with 1/8 cup cheddar cheese on each bake for 15 minutes (if filling is hot) or till the cheese is melted, 20-25 minutes (if the filling is cold). Remove from oven, place on plate garnish with 1 Tbsp. sour cream and 1 Tbsp. tomatoes.

Serve with salsa, enjoy !!

Beef Cubed Swiss Steak
YIELDS: serves 6

6 ea.	Beef cube steak
1 cup	Flour
1 tsp.	Salt
1/2 tsp.	Pepper, black
1/4 tsp.	Garlic, ground
1/4 tsp.	Thyme, ground
1/4 tsp.	Sage, ground
3/4 cup	Oil, vegetable
1 cup	Onion, Spanish, medium diced
1/2 cup	Celery, medium diced
1/2 cup	Carrots, medium diced
1 cup	Green peppers, medium diced
1- 16oz. cn.	Tomatoes, diced with juice
1/2 cup	Tomato paste
2 cup	Beef broth
1/2 cup	Flour

METHOD: Preheat oven 350 degrees F.

Combine in a large bowl 1 cup flour, salt, pepper, garlic, thyme, and sage mix well. Dredge cube steaks in seasoned flour mixture coating completely. Place a sauté pan onto a med-high burner pour in the oil and heat till hot, place dredged cube steaks into the hot pan and brown lightly on each side about 2 to 3 minutes. Place cube steaks into an oven proof baking dish.

Into the sauté pan place onions, carrots, celery, and green peppers stir well and cook till onions become transparent, add 1/2 cup flour, mix well, now add tomato paste and stir well, add diced tomatoes with juice and beef broth stir well and bring to a boil. Then pour this mixture over the cube steaks, cover the baking dish and place into the oven for about 45 minutes or till cube steaks are tender.

Can be served with mashed potatoes, rice pilaf, or pasta.

Country Sausage Gravy
YIELD: 6 servings

2 lb.	Pork, sausage ground
1½ cup	Onion, Spanish, diced fine
¾ cup	Flour, all-purpose
3 cup	Milk, hot
½ tsp.	Pepper, white, ground
12 ea.	Biscuits, pre-made, hot

METHOD:

Place ground pork into a 6 qt. pot and place on a medium-high burner, stirring pork while it is cooking, break up any large pieces and cook till lightly browned. Add onions and cook till onions turn transparent. Now add flour stirring well. Slowly add hot milk and stir till smooth, add pepper and reduce heat. Simmer for 5- 6 minutes and then serve over hot biscuits.

Stir Fry
Beef or Chicken
YIELD: serves 6

1/2 cup	Sesame oil
3 cups	Beef sirloin, or
	Chicken breast, julienne
1/2 cup	Broccoli, flourettes
1/2 cup	Cauliflower, flourettes
1/2 cup	Carrots, julienne
1/2 cup	Bamboo shoots
1/2 cup	Pea pods
2 Tbsp	Soy sauce
1 Tbsp.	Corn starch
1/4 tsp.	Ginger, ground
1/4 tsp.	Garlic, chopped
1/2 cup	Water, cold
3 cup	Rice, white, cooked, hot

METHOD:

Place the sauté pan on a high temperature burner and heat pan then add sesame oil. When hot add beef or chicken stir in pan for 3to 5 minutes or till meat is cooked. Add all vegetables stir well till hot. Mix together in a bowl soy sauce, ginger, garlic, and corn starch then slowly stir in water once mixture is well blended slowly pour into the hot meat and vegetables stir till thickened. Serve over the white rice.

Rock Cornish Hens
YIELD: serves 4

2 ea.	Cornish Hens, thawed, rinsed in cold water
1 ea.	Orange, cut into 8 pieces with peels
2 ea.	Bayleafs, whole
1/4 cup	Onions, Spanish, medium dice
4 ea.	Cloves, whole
1 tsp.	Salt
1/8 tsp.	Pepper, white, ground
1/8 tsp.	Paprika
1 Tbsp.	Butter, melted

METHOD: Preheat oven 350 degrees F.

Into each Cornish Hen cavity place 4 pieces of oranges, 1 bayleaf, 2 cloves, and 1/8 cup onions. Place Cornish Hens into a oven proof baking dish, brush with the melted butter and season with salt, pepper, and sprinkle with paprika. Place into preheated oven and bake for about 1 hour or till an internal temperature is 165 degrees is reached. Remove from oven and let sit for 10 to 15 minutes then cut in half, remove and disgarde onions and oranges.

Serve over wild rice.

Roast Pork Loin Lyonnaise
YIELD: serves 6

3 lb.	Pork loin, boneless, whole
2 cup	Onion, Spanish, julienne
1 Tbsp.	Salt
1 Tbsp.	Pepper, black, coarse grind
1 tsp.	Caraway seed, whole
1/4 tsp.	Garlic, ground
2 cup	Water, cold
1/2 cup	Flour

METHOD: Preheat oven 350 degrees F.

Place the pork loin into a oven proof baking dish, then place onions around the pork loin and sprinkle the salt, pepper, caraway seed, and garlic over the top of pork loin. Place into the preheated oven and roast for about 75 to 90 minutes or till an internal temperature of 165 degrees.

Remove the pork loin from baking dish and place the onions and juices (drippings) into a sauce pan and bring to a boil, reduce the burner heat. Place the flour in a bowl and add the water slowly mixing very well, then pour into the sauce pan stirring well. Increase burner heat, stirring till thickened, then remove from heat. Slice pork loin and serve sauce on the side.

P.S. Lyonnaise is onions in French.

Pork Parmesan
YIELD: serves 4

8 slices	Pork loin, boneless, 1/4" thick slices
1/4 cup	Olive oil
2 cup	Marinara sauce, hot
8 ea.	Mozzarella cheese, sliced 1/8" thick
4 tsp.	Parmesan cheese, grated
24 oz.	Spaghetti, cooked, hot

METHOD: Preheat oven 350 degrees F.

Place a sauté pan on a med-high heated burner, pour in the olive oil and heat up, place pork slices into pan and cook about 2 minutes on each side, remove from pan and place pork into a oven proof baking dish, on each pork slice place 1/4 cup marinara sauce, top sauce with 1 slice of mozzarella cheese, sprinkle 1/2 tsp. Parmesan on top of each slice of cheese. Place into oven till cheese is melted. Serve with spaghetti.

Honey Mustard Glazed Ham
YIELD: serves 6

3 lb.	Ham, canned or small
1 cup	Honey
1/2 cup	Mustard, yellow
12 ea.	Cloves, whole
1/2 cup	Brown Sugar

METHOD: Preheat oven 350 degrees F.

Place ham into a oven proof baking dish then stick cloves into the ham.

Into a mixing bowl combine honey, mustard, and brown sugar stir well. Pour this mixture over the top of ham and place into the oven. Baste the ham every 15minutes with the honey mustard mixture while baking.

Bake for about 11/4 to 11/2 hours or till center of ham has an internal temperature of 155 to 160 degrees F. Remove from oven let ham sit for 10 to 15 minutes before slicing. when sliced serve with sauce poured over the top of ham.

Pork Chops with Peaches
YIELD: 6 Servings

1 - 1 lb. cn.	Peaches, sliced in heavy syrup
6 - 1 inch	Pork chops
2 Tbsp	Vegetable Oil
1 tsp.	Salt
1/4 tsp.	White pepper, ground
1/4 c.	Chili sauce
3 Tbsp.	Lemon juice

METHOD: Preheat oven 350 degrees

Drain peaches, saving the juice. In a large skillet heat vegetable oil. Brown both sides of the chops. Season with salt and pepper. In medium bowl combine 1/3 of peach juice, lemon juice and chili sauce. In oven proof baking dish place chops. Pour chili sauce mix over browned chops. Cover dish with lid place in oven for about 50 to 55 minutes or until tender. Add sliced peaches bake until peaches are hot. Serve.

Herb Baked Cod
YIELD: serves 4

2 lb.	Cod fillets, skinless, boneless
1/2 cup	Butter, melted
2 ea.	Lemons, wedged
1 Tbsp.	Parsley, chopped fine
1/4 tsp.	Tarragon, chopped fine
1/4 tsp.	Thyme, chopped fine
1/2 tsp.	Pepper, black, coarse grind
2 Tbsp.	Onion, Spanish, minced fine

METHOD: Preheat oven 350 degrees F.

Arrange cod fillets into a oven proof baking dish skin side down.(dark side is the skin side of fish) Pour melted butter over cod and sprinkle minced onions over the fillets. Combine the parsley, tarragon, thyme, and black pepper then sprinkle over the fillets and place into preheated oven and bake 20 to 25 minutes or till the fillets are flaky.

Serve with lemon wedges.

Baked Trout Almondine
YIELD: Serves 4

4 ea.	Trout, boneless, headless, whole, 8-10 oz. ea.
1 cup	Butter, melted
1 tsp.	Salt
1/2 tsp.	Pepper, white, ground
1/4 cup	Lemon juice
1 cup	Almonds, sliced, blanched

METHOD: Preheat oven 350 degrees F.

Place a sauté pan onto a med-high heated burner and heat up. Place butter into the pan and melt then add sliced almonds. Stir till almonds turn light brown and remove from heat and set aside.

In a oven proof dish place the trout skin side down sprinkle with seasonings, pour lemon juice on top, now top with the almonds and place into oven and bake 20-25 minutes. Should be flaky when done.

Crab Imperial
YIELD: 4 Servings

1 lb.	Crabmeat, shredded (imitation or real)
1 cup	Mayonnaise
2 Tbsp.	Mustard
Dash	Tabasco
2 Tbsp.	Worcestershire sauce
3 Tbsp.	Lemon juice
3/4 cup	Pimentos, small diced
1 cup	Green pepper, small diced

METHOD: Preheat oven to 350 degrees

In a medium bowl mix all ingredients together. Portion or divide up into 4 balls, flatten out into circular shapes about 1/2" to 3/4" Thick. Place on a baking sheet. Bake until golden brown on top.

15 or 20 minutes. Remove from oven & serve.

Oven Shrimp Scampi
YIELD: 4 Servings

24	Jumbo Shrimp, raw, peeled with tail left on & deveined
4 oz.	Garlic, chopped fine
2 Tbsp.	Fresh Parsley, chopped fine
8 oz.	Butter, sliced thin
1 cup	Fresh bread crumbs
Dash	Black pepper, coarse grind
2 oz.	White wine, dry

METHOD: Preheat oven to 375 degrees

In baking dish lay out cleaned shrimp, sprinkle garlic & parsley over shrimp. Place sliced butter over top & add wine and pepper. Sprinkle bread crumbs over top. Place in preheated oven for 15 to 18 minutes or until shrimp are firm. Serve with rice and fresh French bread.

Can be use in small portion per person as an appetizer.

Pasta
General Cooking Rules

Pasta: almost any type of spaghetti, verminiccili, macaroni, linguini, fettuccini, or egg noodles

Servings: Pasta will double in size and weight

Raw	Cooked	Serves
4oz	8oz	1
8oz	16oz	2
12oz	24oz	3
16oz	32oz	4

Cooking: use 2-3 times the amount of water when cooking pasta
1 gallon of water for every pound of pasta

Sage Stuffing
YIELD: 6 servings

6 cups	Bread; dry, cubed ½" pieces
1 cup	Butter; melted
1½ cup	Onion, spanish; diced fine
1 ½ cup	Celery, diced fine
1 Tbsp.	Sage, whole leaf
½ tsp.	Thyme, leaf
¼ tsp.	Pepper, white, ground
2 each	Chicken, Bouillon Cubes
1 ½ cup	Water, hot

METHOD: Preheat Oven 350 Degrees

Into a sauté pan pour the butter and place on a med-high burner, add onions and celery and cook. Stir frequently, till onions are transparent now add all the spices and stir well.

Dissolve the chicken bouillon cubes in the hot water add to onions and celery mixture, set aside.

Place bread cubes in a mixing bowl and over the top pour the onion and celery mixture stir well, place mixture into an oven-proof baking dish and place in oven for 40 to 45 minutes.

Serve wiht pork, chicken, or turkey and enjoy!!

Rice Pilaf
YIELD: 6 - 1/2 cup servings

2 cup	White Rice
1/4 cup	Butter
1/2 cup	Onion, Spanish, diced fine
1/4 cup	Celery, diced fine
1/4 cup	Carrots, diced fine
2 each	Bayleafs, whole
1/8 tsp.	Thyme, whole
3 cup	Chicken Broth, hot

METHOD:

Place butter into a 2 qt. sauce pot place pot on a med-high burner melt butter then add onions, celery, and carrots cook till the onions are transparent, add rice, bayleafs, thyme stir in very well, add hot chicken broth stir well bring to a boil and then reduce the heat to med-low cover and simmer till the rice is tender.

When the rice is done let set 5-10 minutes, stir well to fluff up the rice before serving.

Fried Rice
YIELD: 6 servings

3 Tbsp.	Sesame Oil
1 cup	Green Peppers, diced fine
1 tsp.	Ginger, fresh, chopped fine
1 tsp.	Garlic, fresh, chopped fine
4 cups	Rice Pilaf (see recipe), Hot
2 Tbsp.	Soy Sauce

METHOD:

Place a 6 Qt. pot on a burner set on high add oil, and heat add green peppers and stir for 30-45 seconds add ginger, garlic, soy sauce and hot rice stir very well and quickly. Serve hot and enjoy.

Cheese & Macaroni
YIELD: 6 servings

1 Qt.	Water
2 cups	Elbow Macaroni
1 Tbsp.	Salt
2 Tbsp.	Butter
1 cup	Milk, hot
1 ½ cup	Velveeta Cheese

METHOD:

Place water and salt into a large pot and place on a med-high burner, bring to a boil. Now add elbow macaroni to boiling water cook till tender. (Do Not Over Cook) Drain and set aside for later use.

To a seperate pot place the butter and put on a med-high burner, when butter is melted add milk heat till hot, slowly add velveeta cheese stirring till smooth, now add the cooked macaroni and stir well. ENJOY!!

Bouillon Potatoes
YIELD: 4 servings

4 ea.   Potatoes, baking, peeled
½ cup   Onions, Spanish, diced fine
2 cup   Chicken broth, hot
2 ea.   Bayleaves
¼ tsp.   Pepper, white, ground

METHOD: Pre-heat oven to 350 degrees.

Place peeled potatoes into a oven proof dish. Sprinkle diced onions over the top of the potatoes, pour the chicken broth into the dish. Add the bayleaves and sprinkle the pepper over potatoes. Cover with aluminum foil and place into the oven and bake for 50-60 minutes or until the potatoes are tender.

Country Style Biscuits

2 cups	All- purpose flour
4 tsp.	Baking powder
1 tsp.	Salt
½ tsp	Baking soda
¼ cup	Bacon grease

Enough butter milk to hold dough together.

METHOD: Preheat oven 375 degrees

In a medium size bowl sift together flour, baking power, baking soda and salt. Make a well in center of flour, add bacon grease, mixing so flour and grease form small clumps. After all flour is clinging to grease, SLOWLY, add butter milk. Just enough to hold dough together. Roll out on a flour surface, about 1/2 inch thick. Cut with a round cutter*. Place on greased flat baking sheet. Bake until golden brown. Brush with butter if desired. Serve warm with honey or jelly.

* Use other simple shapes to cut dough.

Cinnamon Baked Apples
YIELD: 6 servings

6 each	Apples, medium size, core removed
6 tsp.	Raisins
6 Tbsp.	Brown Sugar
½ tsp.	Cinnamon, ground
¼ tsp.	Nutmeg, ground
6 tsp.	Butter

METHOD: Pre-heat oven to 350° degrees.

Mix brown sugar, cinnamon and nutmeg together and set aside.

Place apples into a 10" pie pan then place 1 tsp. of raisins per apple in the core opening top with 1 Tbsp. of brown sugar mixture, top this with 1 tsp. of butter. Place the apples into a pre- heated 350 degree oven for 45-60 minutes, apples should be tender but not mushy.

Serve hot with sauce over them, and enjoy.

Rice Pudding
YIELD: 6 servings

½ cup	Water
½ cup	Rice, white, uncooked
3 ea.	Eggs, whole, whipped lightly
2 tsp.	Vanilla
¼ tsp.	Salt
2½ cup	Milk
½ cup	Raisins
¼ tsp.	Cinnamon, ground

METHOD:

Pre-heat oven to 350 degrees

Mix all the ingredients together well, pour into a buttered 8"x 8" square cake pan. **Bake for 70 minutes or till rice is tender to the bite.** Stir after 20 minutes in the oven.

Raisin Oatmeal Cookies
YIELD: 3 dozen

1 cup	Sugar, white, granulated
1 cup	Brown sugar,
1 cup	Shortening, (vegetable) solid
2 ea.	Eggs, large
1 tsp.	Vanilla
2 cup	Flour, all purpose
1 tsp.	Baking Soda
1 tsp.	Baking Powder
½ tsp.	Salt
2 cup	Quick Cooking Oats
1 cup	Raisins, moist
¼ cup	Apple Sauce

METHOD: Pre-heat oven to 350 degrees.

Cream the sugars and shortening together well, about 3-4 minutes, add eggs, vanilla and mix for 1 minute. Add all other ingredients and mix thoroughly.

Scoop cookies using a number 40 scoop, place about 2" apart on a cookie sheet pan.

Bake for 9-12 minutes, or till slightly golden brown, cool then serve.

Cocoa Mix

2 cups	Powered Milk
1/4 cup	Cocoa, powdered
1 cup	Powered sugar
1/3 cup	Non- dairy creamer
OR	
2 Tbsp	Malted milk

METHOD:

Mix all ingredients together in a reclosable container. Place 3 heaping teaspoons of mix in a cup and add boiling water. Adjust to taste and size of cup. Great with mini marshmallows or whipped cream.

Glossary

AGING: this is applied to meat held at a temperature of 34 to 36 F. to improve it's tenderness.

AU Gratin: food covered with a sauce, sprinkled with bread crumbs or cheese, and baked.

AU JUS: served with natural juices.

AL DENTE: Italian term used to describe food, usually pasta, but also vegetables, cooked so they are firm to the bite.

ALA: in style of.

ALA MODE: usually refers to ice cream on top of pie, but can be other dishes served in a special way.

AVOCADO: a brownish or purple berry filled with a pulp-like marrow, from southern California, tropical America, and West Indies.

BAKING: to cook by moist heat, usually in an oven.

BASTE: to moisten a food product with, stock, product drippings or fat while cooking.

BATTER: mixture of flour and a liquid of a consistency that can be stirred.

BEAT: regular lifting motion to bring mixture to a smooth texture, and often to incorporate air into the mixture.

BÉCHAMEL: a rich cream sauce or white sauce.

BLANCH: 1. to bring food to boiling point, then drain, and cool in ice water.
2. to partially cook.

BLEND: to mix thoroughly two or more ingredients.

BOIL: 1. to cook in liquid at boiling point.
2. term used in some types of meat cookery which is really simmering.

BRAISE: to brown meat or vegetables in a small amount of fat to keep juices within. Cooking is finished in a small amount of liquid in a covered pot on top of the stove or in the oven.

BREADING: 1. to roll food in flour, eggs, and bread crumbs before cooking.
2. a procedure used to describe dry, wet, dry method used for coating a variety of foods.

BRINE: liquid of salt and vinegar for pickling.

BROCHETTE: 1. meat broiled and served on a skewer.
2. a metal pin used to hold meat in place.

BROIL: to cook over or under a direct fire or heat source.

BRUNOISE: cut in fine dice (1/8"x 1/8"x 1/8 ") in size.

CAFE':   coffee

CALORIE: the heat required to raise 1 gram of water 1 degree centigrade.

CALORIES: food value in food. A unit expressing the heat producing or energy producing value of food.

CANADIAN BACON: trimmed, pressed, smoked loin of pork, lean.

CANAPÉ: an appetizer, always prepared on a base, such as bread, toast, crackers or some vegetables.

CASSEROLE: a vessel of earthenware, porcelain, or the like, usually with a cover, in which food may be baked and served; also, food served in such a dish.

CAVIAR: eggs or roe of fish, grey and black, usually sturgeon. Seasoned.
Caviar from salmon is red.

CAYENNE PEPPER: hot seasoning, red and pungent in powder and liquid form.

CLARIFY: 1. to make clear, by adding a clarifying agent which removes suspended particles as in a consommé.
2. to melt butter and have it separate.

COLORS: shades produced by using vegetable dyes; liquids or pastes.

COOKING: it is the processing of a food product to make it more palatable, improve its appearance and supply a valuable nutritional need.

COURT BOUILLON: a preparation of vinegar or wine, water and herb's in which meat or seafood is cooked.

CREAM of TARTAR:potassium bitartrate, a white acid, crystalline substance, used in medicine and cooking.

CROCK: 1. an earthenware pot or jar.
2. a electric pot with a lid and temperature dial used to slow cook a variety of items.

CROUTONS: small pieces of fried or toasted bread used in soups or salads, variety of sizes and shapes can be used.

DEGLAZE: to moisten a roast pan or sauté pan with wine, vinegar, stock or water in order to dissolve caramelized drippings so that they may be used in the sauce.

DICE: to cut into small uniform squares.

DOUGH: the thick, uncooked mass of combined ingredients for bread, rolls, cookies, ect...; usually applied to bread.

DREDGED: to coat with flour or another dry ingredient.

DRIPPINGS: the fat and juice which drops from roasting meats.

DUST: to sprinkle lightly with flour or sugar.

ENCHILADAS: Mexican. Tortillas filled with meat, seafood or cheese. Topped with sauce and baked in an oven.

ENZYMES: a minute substance produced by living organisms which has the power to bring about changes in organic materials.

ESPAGNOLE SAUCE: a basic brown sauce.

EXTRACTS: essence of fruits or spices used as flavorings.

FARINA: the coarsely ground inner portion of hard wheat.

FAT: 1. an oily, yellow or white substance deposited in the cells, under the skin and in various other parts of animal bodies, and also in vegetables.

2. a term used for animal or vegetable fat used in cookery.

FERMENTATION: the chemical changes of an organic compound due to action of living organisms, as yeast, producing the formation of leavening gas, carbon dioxide.

FILET: 1. the tenderloins of beef, veal, lamb, mutton or pork without the bone.

2. a piece of fish that has been taken off the bone.

FLEURON: puff pastry baked in a crescent shape, used as a garnish.

GARNISH: 1. to decorate food.

2. referring to a foodstuff being used to garnish.

GELATIN: 1. the tasteless, odorless brittle substance extracted by boiling bones, hoofs and animal tissues.

2. a granular or sheet like product which is used to thicken a liquid.

GRIDDLE: a heavy plate or pan, broad and shallow for cooking pancakes ect...

GRILL: a frame work of metal bars or wires from which the fire or heat source comes from below the product being cooked.

GUMBO: (SOUP) with meat or seafood, onions, okra, green peppers and tomatoes.

HERB: a large number of aromatic plants used in the kitchen come under the general heading of Herb's.

HORS D OEUVRES: small relishes or appetizers. Served as a first course of the meal.

HUSH PUPPIES: southern deep fat fried dish of corn meal, baking powder, milk, onion and seasoning.

ICE CREAM: a food consisting of cream, butterfat, or milk, and sometimes eggs, sweetened, flavored, beaten to a uniform consistency, and frozen.

INFUSION: liquid obtained from steeping a food, spice, flower or plant. This has become popular in recent years.

JULIENNE: cut into long slices, but thin. (1/8 "x 1/8"x1~1 1/2")

KOSHER: 1. meat sold within 48 hours after butchering in accordance with prescribed Hebrew religious laws.
2. style of cooking adhering to Jewish dietary restrictions.

LARD: 1. the fat of hogs, after being melted from the flesh.
2. to insert strips of salt pork into lean meat with a larding needle.

LEAVENING: the action of carbon dioxide, yeast, baking powder, or baking soda and sour milk.

LIAISON: a rich binding agent, usually cream and egg yokes.

LYONNAISE: with onion.

MARBLING: the amount of fatty connective tissue mixed between the lean meaty parts of an animal.

MEAT: a term used to define beef, veal, pork, poultry or seafood; a generalized term.

MIREPOIX: mixture of onions, celery, carrots used to flavor soups, stocks, sauces, stews and roasted meats or poultry.

MIXING: uniting two or more ingredients.

PAPAYA: a tropical fruit, the juice of which yields an enzyme used as a meat tenderizer.

PAR BOIL: to boil raw food until partially cooked.

PASTA: the flour pasta or dough used in making spaghetti, macaroni, ravioli, ect...

PASTEURIZED MILK: milk held at 140 degrees F. for 30 minutes to destroy potentially harmful microbes.

PASTRY BAG: a cone shaped bag with a metal tip put inside it at the small end. Used to decorate cakes mainly, but can be used for other items also.

PETITE: small.

PILAF: rice cooked in stock with onions, celery, carrots, herb's and spices.

POACHING: cooking in water that bubbles lightly, simmering at 205 degrees F.

POUND: a unit of measure, 16 ounces.

POUNDING: the act of beating using a mallet to tenderize or pulverize a food item.

PROOFING: the process of which dough rises.

PUREE: 1. pulp or paste of vegetable, fruit or meat item.
2. type of soup which is thick

RAISINS: dried out grapes.
REDUCE: 1. to turn down the heat source.
               2. a method used to reduce volume by cooking or simmering.
RENDERING: to free fat from the connective tissues by heat.
ROASTING: to cook in the oven by dry -heat.
ROOT: name used for a category of vegetable, plants, any underground parts.
ROULADE: a rolled piece of thinly sliced meat.
ROUX: equal parts of fat and flour cooked, used to thicken soups, sauces and gravies.
SAUCE: a liquid or soft dressing served with food to improve its taste.
SAUTÉ: to cook quickly in a small amount of fat. To jump.
SCALE: an instrument used for weighing food and ingredients.
SCORE: to score is to make incisions forming a pattern on cakes or pies.
SEARING: to brown the surface of meat quickly by intense heat, in a pan on the stove or under the broiler.
SEED: the part of a flowering plant that contains the embryo and will develop into a new plant if sown.
SIMMERING: slow cooking at just below boiling from 205 to 210 degrees F.
SKEWER: a long pin like utensil to hold meat, vegetables or fruit. made of metal or wood.
SKIM: the process of removing scum or grease accumulated on the surface of a soup, sauce or stock using a skimmer or ladle.
SMOOTHER: to cook vegetables in covered kettle until tender.
SOUFFLÉ: light puffed baked custard, consisting of a sauce and egg yoke mixture to which a puree or flavoring is added and into which stiffly beaten egg whites are gently folded.
SOUP: a liquid food made by cooking meat, fish, vegetables ect..., in water, milk ect...
SOY SAUCE: made from soy beans. Brown. For flavoring Chinese food.
SPICES: aromatic vegetable substances (dry) for flavorings.
SPIT: a pointed rod to hold meat or poultry for roasting in front of or over a fire.
STEAMING: cooking in steam in an enclosed chamber.
STEEPING: to soak in liquid below boiling point to extract flavor or color, as for tea.

STERILIZING: destroying bacteria and microorganisms by boiling water, heat or steam.

STEW: cooking in liquid or sauce with accompanying vegetables and meat.

STIRRING: mixing food in a circular motion.

STOCK: the liquid in which meat, poultry, fish or vegetables have been cooked.
Either brown or white in color.

TEMPERATURE: degree of heat or cold.

TEMPERING: adjusting temperature of ingredients to a certain degree.

TEXTURE: interior grain or structure of a baked product as shown by a cut surface; the feeling of a substance under the fingers.

THERMOMETER: an instrument for measuring temperature.

VELOUTE: 1. soup; a cream soup to which a liaison is added in addition to a puree of the desired garnish.
2. sauce; a thick creamy sauce made by adding veal stock (and milk) to a bland roux.

YEAST: a microscopic fungus(plant) which reproduces by budding and causes fermentation and the giving off of carbon dioxide.

About the Author

R. Bruce Laudermilk graduated from the Culinary Institute of America, Hyde Park, New York, September of 1976. He has worked in the service industry at hotels, country clubs, and resorts, throughout the United States. Progressing to the position of Food and Beverage Director. The early years were spent as an apprentice at Colonial Williamsburg, Virginia, where he was impressed by Marcel Desaulnier's persistence on having sound knowledge of the basics. What became apparent after working at various properties was the need to return to teaching the basics. This enabled the author to develop good cooks to highly competent chefs. Teaching the basics is still his foundation, which is the reason he wrote this book.

Contact Author at ABCALA1@ TDS.NET